German Romantic Motets

Brahms, Bruckner, Cornelius and Mendelssohn

Selected and edited by
Ralph Allwood

Phrase by phrase translations by
Elizabeth Robinson

Novello

Published in Great Britain by
Novello Publishing Limited

Head Office:
Novello & Company Limited
8/9 Frith Street, London W1D 3JB, England.
Telephone: +44 (0)20 7434 0066
Fax: +44 (0)20 7287 6329

Sales & Hire:
Music Sales Limited
Newmarket Road, Bury St Edmunds,
Suffolk IP33 3YB, England.
Telephone: +44 (0)1284 702600
Fax: +44 (0)1284 768301

Music setting by Chris Hinkins.

Front cover painting:
Gothic Cathedral by the Water, 1813,
Karl Friedrich Schinkel. Courtesy of AKG Images.
Back cover photograph:
Ralph Allwood by Tom Allwood. www.tomallwood.com

NOV078639
ISBN 0-7119-9846-9

e-mail: music@musicsales.co.uk
www.chesternovello.com

Abendlied: German Romantic part-songs and anthems,
sung by the Rodolfus Choir conducted by Ralph Allwood,
is available on Herald AV Publications (HAVPCD 289).

Other anthologies by Ralph Allwood
available from Novello:
By Popular Request NOV072524
By Special Arrangement NOV072523
Russian Choral Masterpieces NOV310801

Contents

Notes on the music

Johannes Brahms

Geistliches Lied

The revival of aesthetic interest in older music was a key feature of the nineteenth century, whereas in the previous century old music had been studied, if at all, purely to learn technical proficiency. Brahms was a leader in the new movement. While a young man in the 1850s, he became fascinated by the music of Palestrina and Bach, and wrote a number of canonic pieces – including a Mass that he later reworked as *Warum ist das Licht gegeben*. *Geistliches Lied* is another example of this process – the voice parts form a canon 4 in 2 (soprano and tenor imitate each other, alto and bass likewise), the organ part often in the same style. Such is Brahms's skill in creating arching phrases, however, that the result is anything but dry; rather it is an unfolding of lyricism that perfectly matches the soothing consolation of its text, rising nevertheless to a thrilling climax on the last page.

Ich aber bin elend

The other Brahms pieces in this collection date from thirty years later in his career. The contrapuntal rigour is still present in the eight-part writing, but has now been absorbed with seamless mastery into his natural style. Brahms compiled the text of *Ich aber bin elend* from Exodus and the Psalms. Though not a conventional practising Christian, he was fond of creating his own texts from biblical sources, the best-known example being the *Requiem*. The darkly intense opening section, with its striking use of expressive dissonance, graphically expresses the writer's misery. This gives way to purer harmony and an antiphonal texture to express God's goodness; and the aspects of these two styles finally fuse towards the close, with the writer now confident of an answer to his cry for help.

Unsere Väter hofften auf dich

The *Fest- und Gedenksprüche* Op. 109 were completed in 1889 and served as resources for the celebration of national holidays: thus the Old Testament texts reflect social and national themes, and may indeed echo Brahms's own feelings. The idiom often betrays the influence of Schütz, particularly in its use of an antiphonal double choir. In *Unsere Väter*, God's protection of his people is expressed from the outset in a warm and confident F major, with strong unison passages answered by flowing lines. The writing then becomes progressively more animated at the words 'Zu dir schrieen sie' ('They cried to thee').

Wo ist ein so herrlich Volk

The last of the Op. 109 triptych is written on a grand scale: Brahms here achieves
a coherent structure that is nonetheless alert to the text. The texture at the opening
is wonderfully sonorous; and the presentation of the words, with its invigorating
opening line, is expansive. Brahms halts the flow, however, at 'Hüte dich nur'
('Only look after yourself') and proceeds with a more thoughtful declamation,
which gathers momentum at the mention of 'Geschichte' ('history') and its national
associations.

Anton Bruckner

Christus factus est

With Bruckner's motets, we enter a more intense sound-world: dramatic gestures,
extremes of range and dynamic, interspersed with passages of rarefied polyphony.
Sacred choral music was central to Bruckner's creative life and to his work as a church
organist, so it is no surprise that his motets should be so effective and powerful.
The three here were written around the same time near the beginning of his period
in Vienna. Many would cite *Christus factus est* as the most powerful of all these
motets. Bruckner rises to the challenge of his Passiontide text in a setting full of choral
richness, which nevertheless leaves the impression of starkness, even desolation.
The texture contrasts closely spaced homophony with polyphony that achieves a
'sinewy' effect through unexpected spacing and the use of a fifth as part of several of
the lines. Like much of Bruckner's work, it relies on a generous acoustic and a choir
of substantial tone to achieve its full effect.

Pange lingua

Pange lingua is rarely sung, a motet in self-consciously archaic style which shows
the influence of the Cecilian movement of the time, with its advocacy of harmonic and
contrapuntal purity. The piece hints at modality, and suggests plainsong in the outline
of the opening soprano and alto lines. Yet even here Bruckner cannot resist one or
two dramatic contrasts of dynamic. The sustained effect, harder to maintain vocally
than it might sound, is not unlike that of an organ prelude, such as Bruckner must
have improvised many times.

Locus iste

Locus iste, designed for the dedication of a church but widely applicable within a
liturgical context, is among the simplest of Bruckner's motets but lacks nothing in
intensity. Its success, like so many of Mozart's apparently 'simple' and spontaneous
creations, lies in the careful balancing of four-bar phrases, themselves comprising
two-bar segments, and the use of modulations away from C major that are the more
effective for being sparing.

Virga Jesse

Virga Jessa is less well known than many of the other motets in this collection, yet it is no less effective or resonant. It most nearly approaches the composer's symphonies in its spaciousness (several bars longer than *Christus factus est*) and in the insistent development of a single motif – in this case the dotted figure heard cadentially in bar 9, which assumes greater prominence from bar 37, and then is transformed, almost scherzo-like, into the 'Alleluia' of the closing section from bar 63. Familiar hallmarks are here, in particular the contrast between the pure linear style of the opening and the striking chordal gestures such as bar 23. Bruckner makes telling use of the interval of a sixth, whether rising (bar 22-3 and ff.) or falling (bar 52 ff.).

Peter Cornelius

Bußlied

Cornelius was an exact contemporary of Bruckner. He was at various times personal assistant to both Liszt and Wagner; an ambivalent but important member of the New German School with its forward-thinking aesthetics of Romanticism; and a poet, thinker and composer (he called himself a 'Dichter-Musiker'). The 3 *Psalmlieder* are a work of Cornelius' maturity. By then he had moved away from the New German School and was experimenting with historical models, part of the assimilation of the past that we also see in the work of Mendelssohn and Brahms. Whereas *Die Könige* employs an old chorale as a backdrop, these pieces are, intriguingly, arrangements of Bach dance movements to Cornelius' own paraphrases of psalm texts. It is not clear whether he chose the musical models first, and then selected psalms to fit, or vice versa, but the practical success of the concept is undeniable. In *Bußlied*, the balancing of verbal phrases is exactly matched by the Sarabande from Bach's French Suite No. 1, BWV 812, while the many feminine endings serve as a vehicle for the psalmist's repeated and apparently unanswered questions.

Jerusalem

The third of these Bachian 'psalm-paraphrases' is of Psalm 122 (*I Was Glad*), known to most musicians today through Parry's grandiloquent setting, but set here to endearingly modest music – the brief Second Minuet from Bach's keyboard Partita no. 1, repeated twice. Cornelius makes his view of the piece clear in his footnote, affirming Bach's intentions as 'majesty and dignity'. Certainly the choral version makes a stirring effect as instructed, even if one might envisage something more intimate in the keyboard original!

Die Könige (The Kings)

Out of a substantial and little known output consisting mainly of choral music
and songs, *Die Könige* (The Kings) has become by far Cornelius's best known work.
It is often sung in English as an Epiphany carol although the original, one of the
6 *Weihnachtslieder* Op. 8 from 1856, was a solo song with piano accompaniment.
The choral version remains equally successful and enables the listener to appreciate
more clearly the skilful dovetailing of Cornelius's solo melody with Philipp Nicolai's
chorale 'Wie schön leuchtet der Morgenstern'. The use of instrumental accompaniment,
with its repeated quaver chords in bars 18-21 and 25, adds an extra intensity to the
later sections.

Stromflut

For the third of the *Psalmlieder*, Cornelius set his highly coloured version of
Psalm 137 to another Bach Sarabande, this time from the G minor English Suite, a
movement with an almost obsessive quality to the harmony, rhythm and melody.
It is an apt choice for a psalm expressing the frustrated longing of exile. Cornelius
further intensifies the music, by his instructions to accelerate during the second stanza,
in which the music of the first is repeated, and then slows dramatically for the
conclusion: 'nur beim Heimgang' ('only at death').

Die Vätergruft

This was one of Cornelius's last works before his unexpected death from diabetes.
The unusual texture, solo baritone supported by four-part chorus, provides a rationale
for the arrangement of *Die Könige*; the scoring was originally for SABB but can
be sung in various combinations including by men's voices ATBarB (considering its
subject), or transposed upwards by a tone and the solo sung by a low tenor. In this
case, the poem was from another hand, Ludwig Uhland, and is a typical Gothic-
Romantic narrative of a mediaeval knight going to his final rest in an ancient chapel.
The choral voices represent the spirits of former knights, welcoming the newcomer
to their ranks. From bar 24, the music modulates impulsively, perhaps conveying the
knight's eagerness to join the company. Solo and chorus become increasingly
integrated, until the last page where silence gradually falls, leaving the solo voice to
hang unsupported.

Felix Mendelssohn

Am Karfreitage

Mendelssohn's six motets, or *Sprüche*, Op. 79 date from his time as General Music
Director in Berlin during the early 1840s, when he had a brief to revitalize musical life
in the city. Part of this involved the reconstitution of the cathedral choir, for whom
he wrote these brief and charming motets for use in the liturgy at different seasons.
King Wilhelm IV, under the influence of the Cecilian movement (which can also be
discerned in certain Liszt and Bruckner works), had decreed a return to the Palestrina
a cappella style. A still more intriguing comparison with Bruckner arises with this piece,
setting as it does the same text as the latter's *Christus factus est* of forty years later.
Indeed even the harmonic progression of the first three bars is similar, leading
us to wonder whether Bruckner unconsciously took Mendelssohn's setting as a point
of departure for his own. Certainly the contrast between the low setting of 'Kreuze'
('cross') and the forte block chords, an octave higher, of 'darum hat Gott ihn erhöhet'
('because of this, God has exalted him') is the nearest Mendelssohn comes in these
motets to the drama of Bruckner's works. The Alleluia is brief and telling.

In der Passionszeit

This Passiontide setting is even more restrained: it is almost as though it gains a
sombre focus through its simplicity rather than through any overt display of anguish.
All these motets conclude with an Alleluia, extensive in the celebratory *Weihnachten*,
somewhat more muted, for obvious reasons, in nos. 4 and 6. There is an intriguing
foretaste of the Alleluia from Bruckner's *Virga Jesse* in the dotted rhythms at the end
of no. 4.

Weihnachten

Mendelssohn's return to the Palestrina *a cappella* style can be appreciated in the
diatonicism and regular flow of *Weihnachten*. Only certain moments of harmonic
richness in the sumptuous eight-part writing betray a nineteenth-century aesthetic.

David Goode

Geistliches Lied

Paul Fleming (1609–40)

Johannes Brahms (1833–97)
Op.30

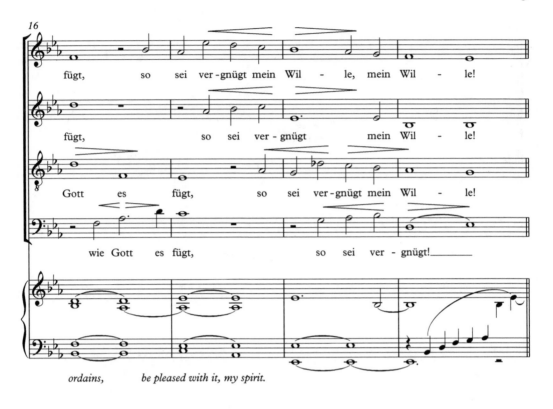

fügt, so sei ver-gnügt mein Wil - le, mein Wil - le!

fügt, so sei ver-gnügt mein Wil - le!

Gott es fügt, so sei ver-gnügt mein Wil - le!

wie Gott es fügt, so sei ver - gnügt!

ordains, be pleased with it, my spirit.

Was willst du heu - te

Was willst du

Was

Man.

Why worry today

about tomorrow? *He who takes care of everything,*

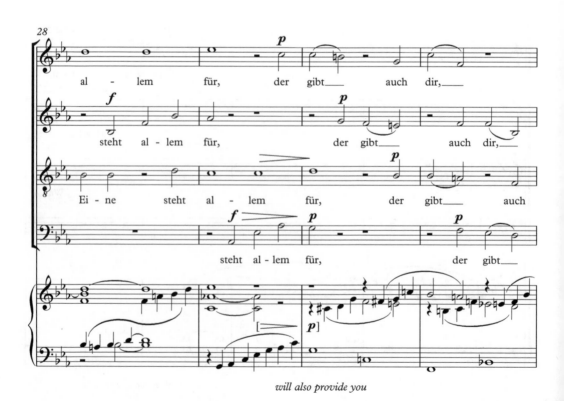

will also provide you

In all your dealings do not waver,

stand firm; what God ordains,

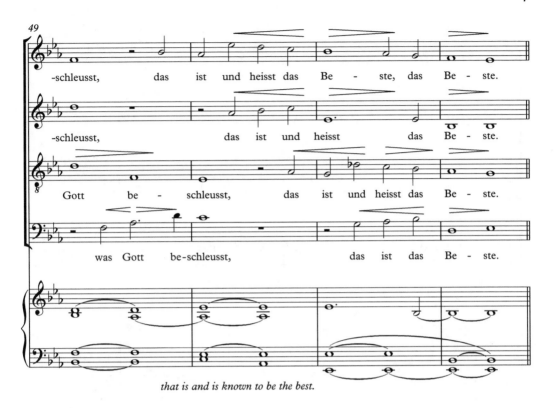

that is and is known to be the best.

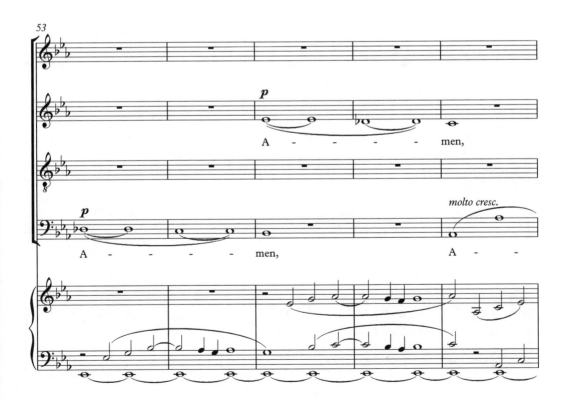

Ich aber bin elend

Psalm 69, vv. 30, 2 and
Exodus ch. 34, vv. 6–7

Johannes Brahms (1833–97)
Drei Motetten, Op. 110, no. 1

But I am miserable and woe is me;

12

Lord God,   merciful and gracious and long-suffering,

and full of grace and truth,

14

showing grace in a thousand ways,   *forgiving iniquity and*

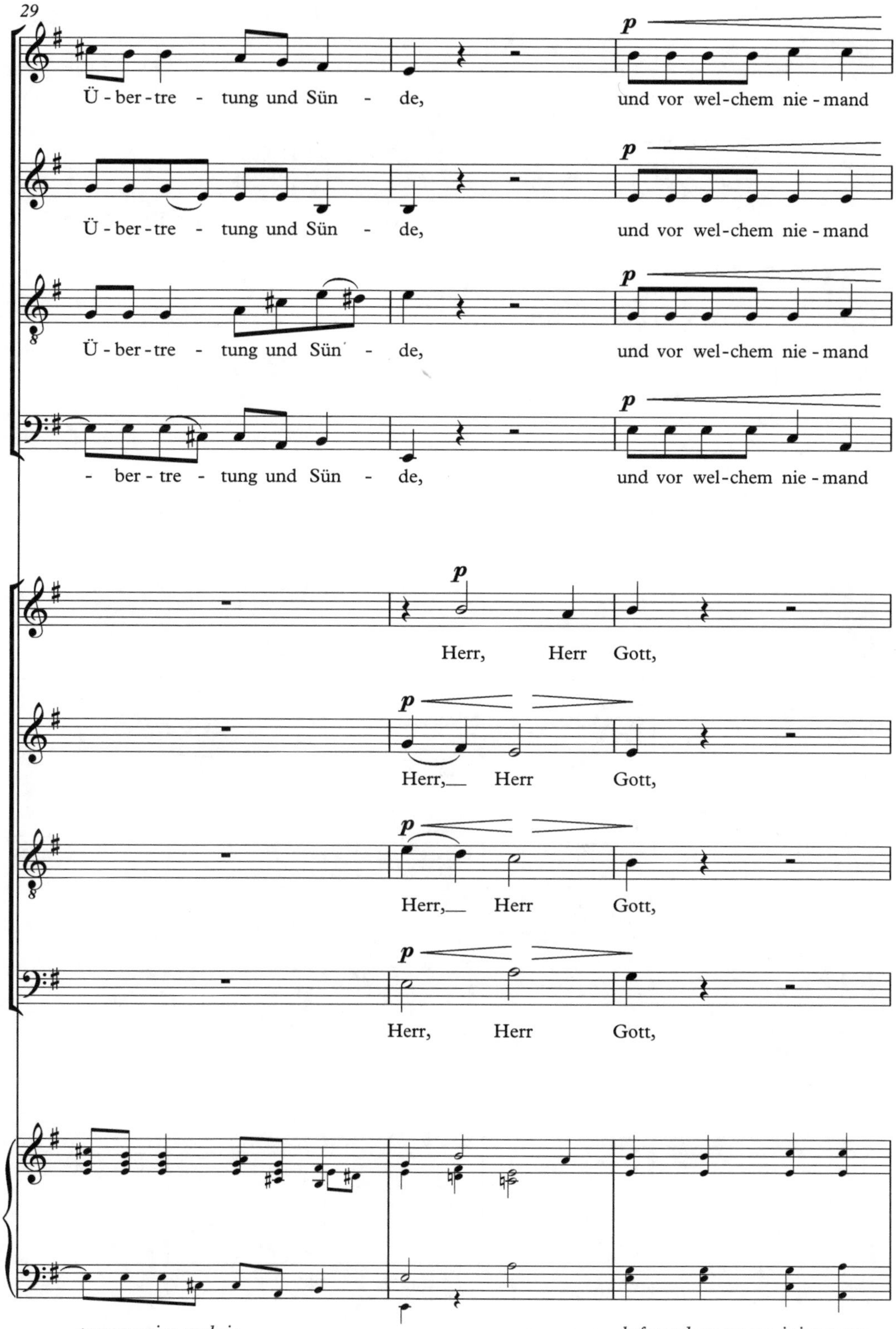

transgression and sin, *before whom no-one is innocent;*

16

God, let thy help protect me.

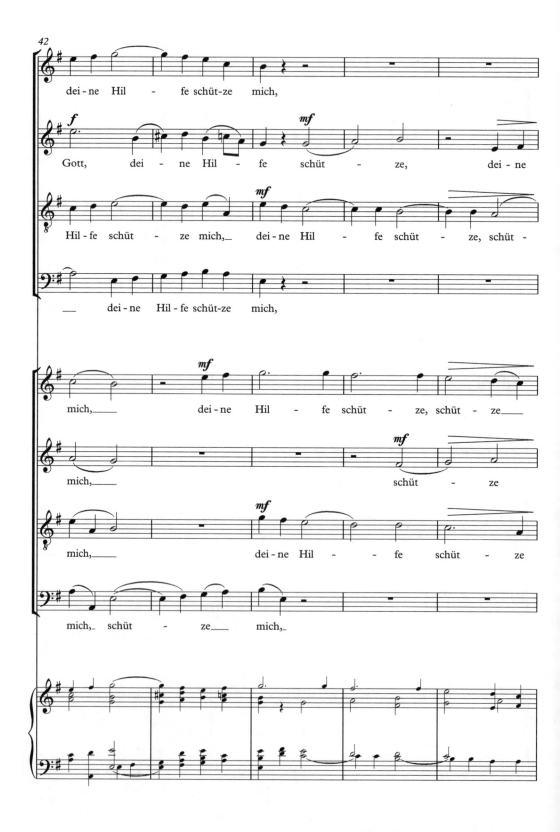

Unsere Väter hofften auf dich

Psalm 22, vv. 4–5;
Psalm 29, v. 11

Johannes Brahms (1833–97)
Fest- und Gedenksprüche, Op. 109, no. 1

hoff - - ten auf dich; und da sie
hoff - - ten auf dich; und da sie
hoff - - ten auf dich; und da sie
hoff - ten auf dich; und da sie

dich; und da sie hoff - ten,
dich; und da sie hoff - ten,
dich; und da sie hoff - ten,
dich; und da sie hoff - ten,

thee: *and since they trusted,*

22

thou didst deliver them.

They cried to thee,   *and*

were saved,

and

were not confounded.

The Lord will give strength to his people;   *the Lord will bless his people*

with peace.

Wo ist ein so herrlich Volk

Deuteronomy ch. 4, vv. 7, 9

Johannes Brahms (1833–97)
Fest- und Gedenksprüche, Op. 109, no. 3

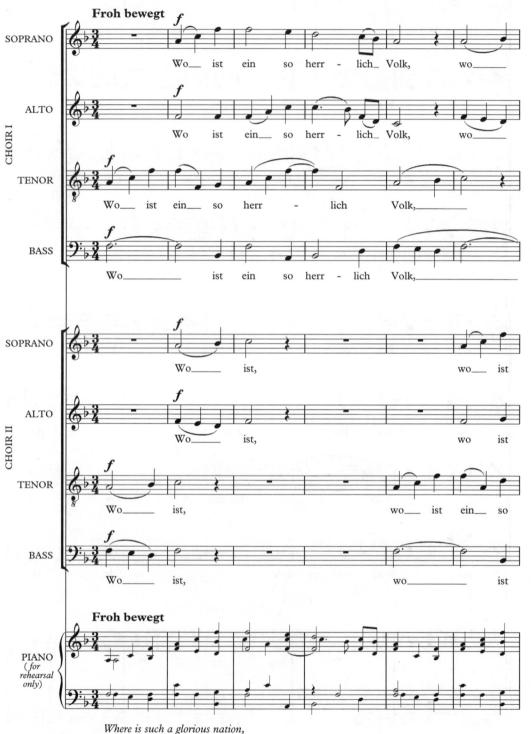

Where is such a glorious nation,

which is as close to the gods

than the Lord, our God,   *as often as we*

call upon him?

Only look after yourself,

and take good care of your soul,

40

lest you forget   *the history*

58

which your eyes have seen,

and that it does not leave your heart

44

all the days of your

life: and make it known to your children

and children's

children.

Christus factus est

Gradual for Maundy Thursday,
Philippians ch. 2, vv. 8–9

Anton Bruckner (1824–96)
Vier Graduale, no. 1

Christ was made obedient unto death for us,

even death

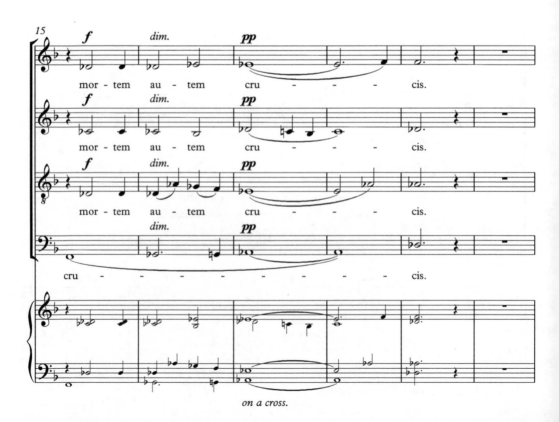

on a cross.

Because of this, God has exalted him

and

given him that name   which is greater

than all other names.

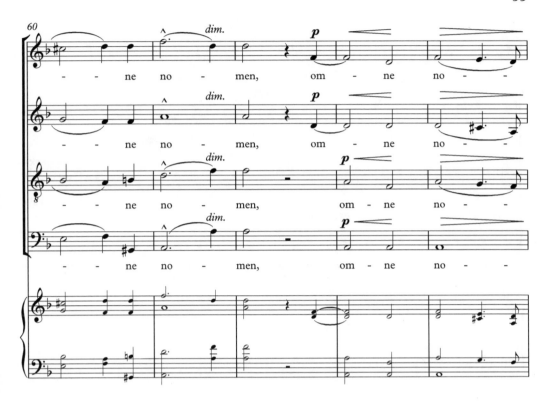

56

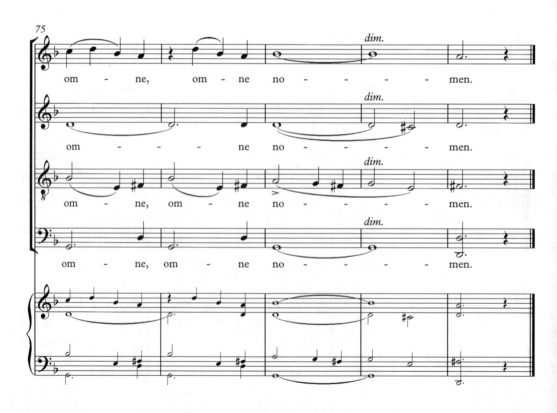

Pange lingua

Hymn of the Corpus Christi office
St. Thomas Aquinas (1227–74)

Anton Bruckner
(1824–96)

Speak out, my tongue, and tell
of the mystery of the glorious Body
and of the precious Blood which the King,
fruit of a generous womb,
As the price of the world,
poured out over mankind. Amen.

Therefore, we, bent to the ground,
venerate this Sacrament
And the ancient rite
Gives way to the new
Faith makes up for what is lacking
To our outward senses.

Let there be praise and glory
To the Begetter and the Begotten
And honour, might and strength
Let there be, and blessing.
To the One proceeding from them both
Let there be equal praise.

Locus iste

Gradual for the mass
for the dedication of a church

Anton Bruckner (1824–95)
Vier Graduale, no. 2

Virga Jesse

Feast of the Blessed Virgin

Anton Bruckner
(1824–96)

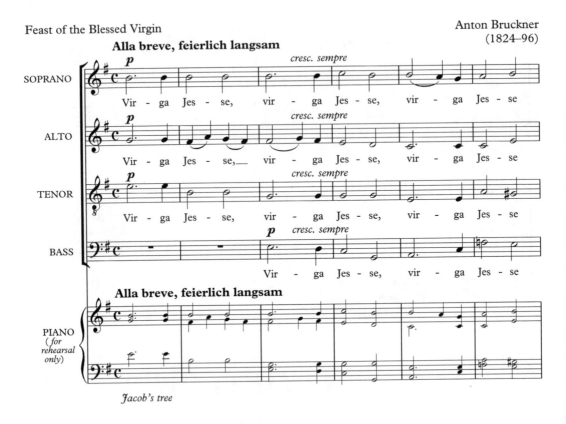

Jacob's tree

has blossomed

A virgin has borne God

and man.

God has restored peace

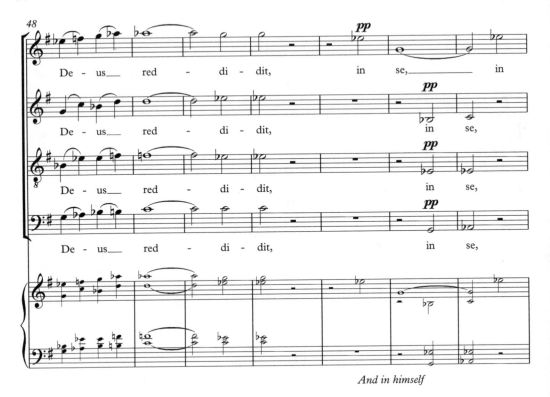

And in himself

has reconciled

the lowest with the highest. Alleluia.

dem Gesangverein in Zittau und dessen Dirigenten Herrn Paul Fischer

Busslied
'Warum verbirgst du vor mir dein Antlitz?'

Peter Cornelius
after Psalm 88

Peter Cornelius (1824–74)
3 Psalmlieder, Op. 13, no. 1
after the Sarabande from Bach's French Suite No. 1

Mässig langsam
[*Andantino*]

Why do you hide your face from me,

Why have you forsaken my soul?

My God, my

saviour, how have I day and night   wept bitter tears

of remorse!

My grief, my laments, are holding me as a prisoner,

72

No   star can relieve the darkness by   dawning.

Desolation, like the   grave,   envelops my heart,

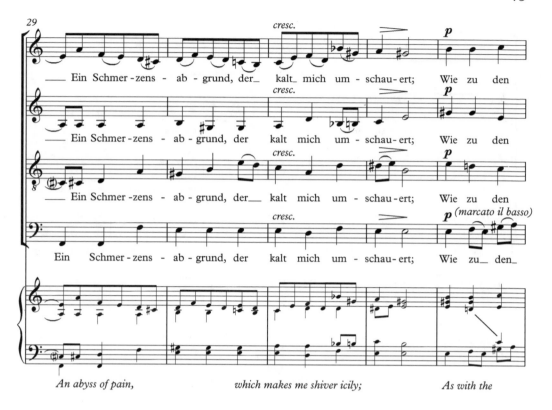

An abyss of pain,   which makes me shiver icily;   As with the

dead,   Lord, you have abandoned me   So that without hope, without comfort,

74

my soul mourns.   *When you, Lord, do not respond to me, what a dreadful*

silence!   When, O God, will you hear my plea?

dem Gesangverein in Zittau und dessen Dirigenten Herrn Paul Fischer

Jerusalem
'Heil und Freude ward mir verheissen'

Peter Cornelius
after Psalm 122

Peter Cornelius (1824–74)
3 Psalmlieder, Op. 13, no. 3
after the 2nd Minuet from Bach's 1st Partita in B♭

* Dies Lied bedarf keiner weiteren Vortragsbezeichnungen, schlicht und grossartig, wie Bach es hinstellte, werde es gesungen.
This song requires no further markings, it will be sung with majesty and dignity as Bach meant it.

Thy temple, Jerusalem!   *High and*

glorious are you built,   *All the nations come to*

24

dir; Got - tes Na-men hörst du ver - kün - den, Hörst ihn

dir; Got - tes Na - men hörst du ver - kün - den, Hörst ihn

dir; Du hörst___ Gott___ laut___ ver - kün - den Und prei-

dir; Got - tes Na - men hörst du ver - kün - den, Hörst ihn

you;   You hear God's name pronounced,   Hear him

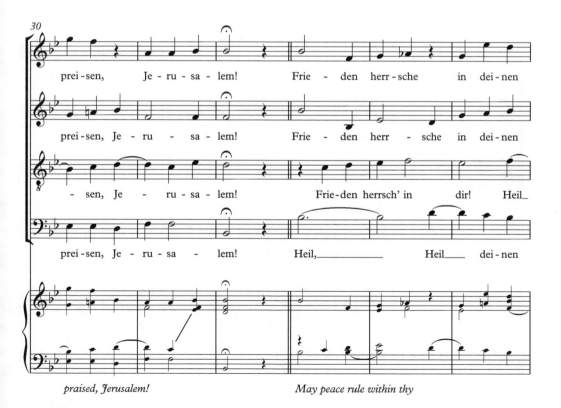

30

prei-sen, Je-ru-sa-lem! Frie - den herr-sche in dei-nen

prei-sen, Je - ru - sa - lem! Frie - den herr - sche in dei-nen

- sen, Je - ru - sa - lem! Frie-den herrsch' in dir! Heil_

prei-sen, Je - ru - sa - lem! Heil,___ Heil___ dei-nen

praised, Jerusalem!   May peace rule within thy

walls,   *Hail to your dwellings, hail to your courts!*   *Hail to the*

hearts,   *which full of love*   *True to you beat,*   *Jerusalem!*

Die Könige
The Kings

Translations: W.G. Rothery (solo text)
William Mercer (Chorale)

Chorale melody by Philipp Nicolai (1556–1608)
Solo melody and German text by Peter Cornelius (1824–74)
Weihnachtslieder, Op. 8 no. 3

This work can be performed by
a) solo voice and piano/organ
b) solo voice and choir or
c) solo voice, choir and piano/organ.

neu - ge - bo - re - ne Kö - nig_ sei? Sie wol - len Weih - rauch, Myr - rhen und
new - born King whom they seek doth_ dwell. Fine gold and myrrh and in - cense they

Wahr - heit von dem_ Herrn, die
beam - ing from a - far; The

Gold dem Kin - de_ spen - den zum Op - fer - sold. Und hell er -
bring, An of - f'ring to the pro - mised new - born_ King. The guid - ing

süs - se Wur - zel_ Jes - - se.
host of heav'n_ re - joi - - ces:

nei - gen die___ Kön' - ge___ sich;
-fore___ him in___ wor - ship___ there.

sie brin - gen Weih-rauch, Myr-rhen und
Fine gold and myrrh and in - cense they

und mein Bräu - ti - gam,
Man and Son of God!

hast
We

Gold zum Op - fer___ dar___ dem Knäb-lein___ hold.___
bring, An of - f'ring to the pro-mised new - born King.___

O Men-schen-kind!
And still the star,

mir mein Herz___ be - ses - sen. Lieb - - -
too, will lift___ our voi - ces: Je - - -

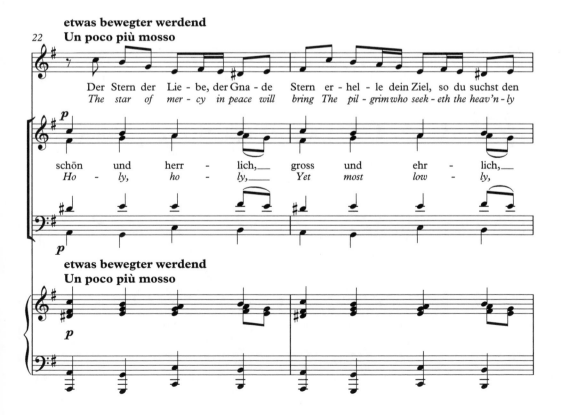

84

Stromflut
'An Babels Wasserflüssen'

Peter Cornelius
after Psalm 137

Peter Cornelius (1824–74)
3 Psalmlieder, Op. 13, no. 2
after the Sarabande from Bach's English Suite No. 3

The river flows through Babylon's meadows: *Heart's blood,*

you burst into tears!   *Zion, you shine brightly in*

agonising   dreams   As   your   nation lost you for ever!

The olive trees grow green for you, the palm trees still wave coolly,

Our hearts break, *and bloom no longer.*

Schneller, mit wachsender Leidenschaft
[*Più allegro, con passione*]

Ignominiously the cry of our enemy besets us: *'Sing to us about*

Zion!' so demands his command; But woe, my people,

endless woe to you, If you sing the Lord's songs to the enemy, who

threatens you!   Once more, only   at death shall your song be sounded

Zion,   O   Zion.

Die Vätergruft

Ludwig Uhland (1787–1862)
and Peter Cornelius

Peter Cornelius (1824–74)
Op. 19

Es ging wohl über die Hai - de Zur al - ten Ka-pell' em -

He went over the heath   Up to the ancient chapel

-por Ein Greis im Waf - fen-ge-schmei - de, Er trat in den dunk-len

An old man clad in armour   He entered the dark

Chor. Die Sär - ge sei - ner___ Ah - nen Stan - den die Hall' ent -

Heil dir!

Heil dir!

Heil dir!

chancel.   The coffins of his forebears   Stood along the hall,

Hail to you!

* This part was originally scored for basses. It may be necessary to double some passages with basses.

From the depths he heard   *A*

wonderful song.   *Heroic, daring striving,*   *Hurry towards heaven!*

92

Battle and victory disappear   In the grave's

'Well have I heard your greetings,   You heroic spirits
silence.   Blessed spirits greet you

94

folded   On his sword and fell asleep;   The sounds of the spirits

died away: And total silence followed.

Am Karfreitage

from the Prussian *Agende,* 1829

Felix Mendelssohn (1809–47)
6 Sprüche [Op. 79, no. 6]

God has exalted him   and given him a name   which is greater

than all other names.   Hallelujah!

In der Passionszeit

from the Prussian *Agende*, 1829

Felix Mendelssohn (1809–47)
6 *Sprüche* [Op. 79, no. 4]

Lord, remember not our wicked deeds,   and have

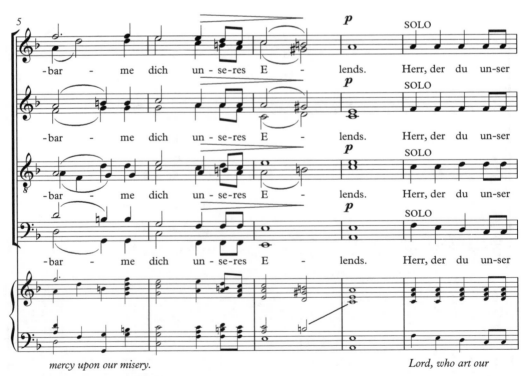

mercy upon our misery.   Lord, who art our

Hallelujah!

from the Prussian *Agende,* 1829

Felix Mendelssohn (1809–47)
6 Sprüche [Op. 79, no. 1]

Rejoice, you people on earth, and praise God!   *The saviour*

has appeared,   whom the

Lord promised.   He has revealed his righteousness to the world.

Hallelujah!

104

123456789

Texts

Geistliches Lied
Paul Fleming (1609-40)
Johannes Brahms, Op. 30, 1856

Lass dich nur nichts nicht dauren
    mit Trauren,
    sei stille,
    wie Gott es fügt,
    so sei vergnügt
    mein Wille!

Was willst du heute sorgen
    auf morgen?
    Der Eine
    steht allem für,
    der gibt auch dir
    das Deine.

Sei nur in allem Handel
    ohn' Wandel,
    steh feste,
    was Gott beschleußt,
    das ist und heißt
    das Beste. Amen.

Ich aber bin elend
Psalm 69, v. 30, 2 & Exodus 34, vv. 6-7
Johannes Brahms, *Drei Motetten*, Op. 110, no. 1, 1889

Ich aber bin elend, und mir ist wehe; Herr Gott, barmherzig und gnädig
und geduldig, und von großer Gnade und Treue, der du beweisest Gnade
in tausend Glied, und vergibst Missetat, Übertretung und Sünde, und
vor welchem niemand unschuldig ist; Gott, deine Hilfe schütze mich.

Unsere Väter hofften auf dich
Psalm 22, vv. 4-5; Psalm 29, v. 11
Johannes Brahms, *Fest- und Gedenksprüche*, Op. 109, no. 1, 1888-9

Unsere Väter hofften auf dich; und da sie hofften, halfst du ihnen aus.
Zu dir schrieen sie, und wurden errettet, und wurden nicht zu Schanden.
Der Herr wird seinem Volk Kraft geben, der Herr wird sein Volk segnen
mit Frieden.

Wo ist ein so herrlich Volk

Deuteronomy ch. 4, vv. 7, 9
Johannes Brahms, *Fest- und Gedenksprüche*, Op. 109, no. 3, 1888-9

Wo ist ein so herrlich Volk, zu dem Götter also nahe sich tun als der Herr,
unser Gott, so oft wir ihn anrufen. Hüte dich nur und bewahre deine Seele
wohl, dass du nicht vergessest der Geschichte, die deine Augen gesehen
haben, und dass sie nicht aus deinem Herzen komme alle dein Leben lang.
Und sollst deinen Kindern und Kindeskindern kund tun. Amen.

Christus factus est

Gradual for Maundy Thursday, Philippians ch. 2, vv. 8-9
Anton Bruckner, *Vier Graduale*, no. 1, 1869

Christus factus est pro nobis obediens usque ad mortem autem crucis.
Propter quod et Deus exaltavit illum, et dedit illi nomen, quod est super
omne nomen.

Locus iste

Gradual from the mass for the dedication of a church
Anton Bruckner, *Vier Graduale*, no. 2, 1869

Locus iste a Deo factus est, inaestimabile sacramentum irreprehensibilis est.

Virga Jesse

Feast of the Blessed Virgin
Anton Bruckner, 1885

Virga Jesse floruit
Virgo Deum et hominem genuit,
pacem Deus reddidit,
in se reconcilians ima summis. Alleluja.

Bußlied

Peter Cornelius (after Psalm 88)
Peter Cornelius, 3 *Psalmlieder*, Op. 13, no. 1, 1872
after the Sarabande from
Bach's French Suite No. 1, BWV 812

Warum verbirgst du vor mir dein Antlitz,
Warum hast du meine Seele verstoßen!
Mein Gott, mein Heiland, wie hab' ich Tag und Nacht
Die heissesten Tränen der Reue vergoßen!
Mich hält wie gefangen mein Leid, mein Klagen,
Kein Stern erlösend im Dunkel will tagen.

Öde, dem Grab gleich, umgibt das Herz mir,
Ein Schmerzensabgrund, der kalt mich umschauert;
Wie zu den Toten hast, Herr, du mich hingelegt,
Dass hoffenslos, trostlos die Seele mir trauert.
Wenn du, Herr, mir schweigest, welch schaurig Schweigen!
Wann meinem Flehen wirst, O Gott, du dich neigen?

Pange lingua

Hymn of the Corpus Christi office,
St. Thomas Aquinas (1227-74)
Anton Bruckner, 1868

Pange lingua gloriosi
corporis mysterium,
sanguinisque pretiosi,
quem in mundi pretium
fructus ventris generosi
rex effudit gentium. Amen.

Tantum ergo sacramentum
veneremur cernui:
et antiquum documentum
novo cedat ritui:
praestet fides supplementum
sensuum defectui.

Genitori, genitoque
laus et jubilatio,
salus, honor, virtus quoque
sit et benedictio:
procedenti ab utroque
compar sit laudatio.

Jerusalem

Peter Cornelius (after Psalm 122)
Peter Cornelius, 3 *Psalmlieder*, Op. 13, no. 3, 1872
after the 2nd Minuet from
Bach's 1st Partita in B flat, BWV 825

Heil and Freude ward mir verheißen,
Eingeh'n werd' ich zum Haus des Herrn;
Deine Schwelle soll ich begrüßen,
Deinen Tempel, Jerusalem!

Hoch und herrlich bist du erbauet,
Alle Völker wandern zu dir;
Gottes Namen hörst du verkünden,
Hörst ihn preisen, Jerusalem!

Frieden herrsche in deinen Mauern,
Heil den Hütten, den Hallen Heil!
Heil den Herzen, die voll von Liebe
Treu dir schlagen, Jerusalem!

Die Könige (The Kings)

Peter Cornelius (1824-74)
Peter Cornelius, *Weihnachtslieder*, Op. 8, no. 3, 1856

Drei Könige wandern aus Morgenland;
ein Sternlein führt sie zum Jordanstrand.
In Juda fragen und forschen die Drei,
wo der neugeborene König sei?
Sie wollen Weihrauch, Myrrhen und Gold
dem Kinde spenden zum Opfersold.

Und hell erglänzet des Sternes Schein;
zum Stalle gehen die Kön'ge ein;
das Knäblein schauen sie wonniglich,
anbetend neigen die Kön'ge sich;
sie bringen Weihrauch, Myrrhen und Gold
zum Opfer dar dem Knäblein hold.

O Menschenkind! halte treulich Schritt!
Die Kön'ge wandern, O wandre mit!
Der Stern der Liebe, der Gnade Stern
erhelle dein Ziel, so du suchst den Herrn,
und fehlen Weihrauch, Myrrhen und Gold,
schenke dein Herz dem Knäblein hold!
Schenk' ihm dein Herz!
(chorale)
Wie schön leuchtet der Morgenstern
voll Gnad' und Wahrheit von dem Herrn,
die süße Wurzel Jesse.
Der Sohn Davids aus Jakobs Stamm,
mein König und mein Bräutigam,
hast mir mein Herz besessen.
Lieblich, freundlich,
schön und herrlich,
gross und ehrlich,
reich an Gaben,
hoch und sehr prächtig erhaben.

Stromflut

Peter Cornelius (after Psalm 137)
Peter Cornelius, *3 Psalmlieder*, Op. 13, no. 2, 1872
after the Sarabande from
Bach's English Suite No. 3, BWV 808

Stromflut dahin rauscht durch Babels Gefilde:
Herzblut, so brichst du in Tränen hervor!
Zion, du strahlst hell in qualvolle Träume,
Da doch dein Volk dich auf ewig verlor!
Dir grünt der Oelbaum, kühl weht dir die Palme noch,
Uns brach das Herz, blühet nie mehr empor.

Schmachvoll bedrängt uns der Ruf unsres Feindes:
'Singt uns von Zion!' so heischt sein Gebot;
Doch Weh, mein Volk, dir unendlich Wehe,
Sängst du des Herrn Lied dem Feind, der dir droht!
Einmal zuletzt nur beim Heimgang ertön' einst
Zion, O Zion, dein Lied noch im Tod.

Die Vätergruft

Ludwig Uhland (1787-1862)
Peter Cornelius, Op. 19, 1874

Es ging wohl über die Heide
Zur alten Kapell' empor
Ein Greis in Waffengeschmeide,
Er trat in den dunklen Chor.

Die Särge seiner Ahnen
Standen die Hall' entlang,
Aus der Tiefe tät ihn mahnen
Ein wunderbarer Gesang.

Heil dir! Heil dir!

Heldenkühnes Streben,
Eil' dem Himmel zu!
Kampf und Sieg entschweben
In des Grabes Ruh'.

Sel'ger Geister Grüßen
Sehnlich dein begehrt,
Unsre Reih'n zu schließen,
Heil! Du bist es wert.

'Wohl hab ich euer Grüßen,
Ihr Heldengeister, gehört,
Eure Reihen soll ich schließen.
Heil mir! Ich bin es wert!'

Es stand an kühler Stätte
Ein Sarg noch ungefüllt;
Den nahm er zum Ruhebette,
Zum Pfühle nahm er den Schild.

Die Hände tät er falten
Auf's Schwert und schlummert ein;
Die Geisterlaute verhallten:
Da mocht' es gar stille sein.

Am Karfreitage
from the Prussian *Agende*, 1829
Felix Mendelssohn [Op. 79, no. 6], 1844

Um unsrer Sünden willen hat sich Christus erniedriget und ist gehorsam
geworden bis zum Tode am Kreuze; darum hat Gott ihn erhöhet und ihm
einen Namen gegeben, der über alle Namen ist. Halleluja!

In der Passionszeit
from the Prussian *Agende*, 1829
Felix Mendelssohn [Op. 79, no. 4], 1844

Herr, gedenke nicht unsrer Übeltaten, und erbarme dich unseres Elends.
Herr, der du unser Heiland bist, stehe uns bei, erlöse uns und vergieb uns
unsere Sünden um der Herrlichkeit deines Namens willen. Halleluja!

Weihnachten
from the Prussian *Agende*, 1829
Felix Mendelssohn [Op. 79, no. 1], 1843

Frohlokket, ihr Völker auf Erden, und preiset Gott!
Der Heiland ist erschienen, den der Herr verheißen.
Er hat seine Gerechtigkeit der Welt offenbaret. Halleluja!